아라메 둘레길
운산에서 서산으로

Arame Pathway
Through Unsan to Seosan

아라메 둘레길 운산에서 서산으로
Arame Pathway Through Unsan to Seosan
심재황 제8시집

2023년 11월 30일 제1판 인쇄 발행

지은이 | 심재황
펴낸이 | 심재황
펴낸곳 | 도서출판 나리북스

등록번호| 542-12-01995 (2022년 02월 08일)
주소 | 15802 경기도 군포시 고산로 677번길 34, 1324-1303
대표전화| 031) 398-5610
팩스 | 031) 398-5610
이메일 | julyshim@hanmail.net
ISBN 979-11-979286-4-2 (03800)
가격 10,000원

※ 잘못 만들어진 책은 바꿔드립니다.
ⓒ 이 책 내용의 일부 또는 전부를 재사용하려면
반드시 저작권자의 동의를 받아야 합니다.

아라메 둘레길
운산에서 서산으로

Arame Pathway
Through Unsan to Seosan

심재황　제8시집

나리북스

작가의 말

　바닷가 서산 쪽으로 가려다가 동쪽에 산줄기가 보이기에 그곳으로 들어갑니다. 운산 고장에 잠시 들러서 겨우 몇 걸음 지나니 읍내를 벗어나고, 들길과 산길로 들어가게 됩니다.
　그곳에는 남쪽 가야산에서부터 상왕산, 수정봉 줄기가 이어지고 있습니다. 산줄기 아래는 마을과 터전 그리고 다정한 분위기가 남겨져 있습니다.
　여기에서 아라메 둘레길이 시작됩니다. 마을들을 이어주는 산길, 들길, 냇가를 지나며, 남쪽 해미와 서쪽 바다까지 둘러져 있습니다.
　다른 지역과 마찬가지로 골짜기마다 살아오던 분들도 많이 떠나시고, 모습도 바뀌었습니다. 하지만 아직 정겨운 이야기들이 남아있을지 모른다는 생각이 들기도 합니다.
　그런데 지나가다 보면 어떤 이야기가 떠오르기도 하고, 어떤 기억이 되살아나기도 합니다. 그때 친근하던 분과 지나가던 곳일지도 모르고요. 그러기에 아라메 둘레길은 아름다운 이야기가 만들어지는 곳인가 봅니다.

2023년 한여름과 가을에

Author's Note

Heading toward the seaside in Seosan, I chanced to see a mountain range of the east. Stepping into the province of Unsan for a while, I was out of the small town going to the field and the path.

There, the ridges of Sangwangsan and Sujeongbong Peak rise from Gayasan Mountain in the south. Under the range, villages may leave the deep feeling of affection.

The Aramegil pathway begins from the village. It passes through mountain paths, field roads, streams, and villages. It leads to Haemi in the south and the sea in the west.

As in other regions, people who had lived in valleys left. But it makes me think that there may still be some heartwarming stories left.

However, certain stories come to mind and certain memories come back. It may be a place I have passed by before. Therefore, Aramegil pathway is a place where beautiful stories are created.

In midsummer and fall, 2023

감사의 글

　아름다운 고장은 언제나 발길을 끌게 마련입니다. 더구나 어려운 일이 있을 때, 마음에 두고 있는 곳으로 발길이 가게 됩니다.

　봄이 지나고 더운 여름에 잠시 들길을 둘러보려는데. 비가 내려서 돌아오게 됩니다.

　한여름에 다시 들러봅니다. 그런데 또 비가 내리는데 이번에는 한적한 산길로 들어가는데, 가을이 보이기 시작합니다.

　그곳의 아름다운 정경들을 처음으로 들려주신, 카페 '르비딤 (Rephidim)'의 김이라 자매님께 깊고 깊은 감사를 드립니다.

　이라 자매님은 아름다운 서산, 해지는 서산을 말씀하셨습니다. 그리고 "아라메 길"을 따라서 동쪽 지역인 운산과 남쪽 해미 지역을 소개해 주셨습니다.

　겨울에도 이라 자매님이 말씀하신 "아라메 둘레길"을 누군가 설어가게 될 것입니다.

2023년 한여름 그리고 가을에,
저자 드림

Acknowledgments

A beautiful place always attracts visitors. Moreover, when something hard time happens, we are going to the place we have in mind.

In summer, I was planning to take a quick look around the field. However, it rained so hard, so I came back.

I dropped by again in hot summer. I have caught in the rain again. This time, as I entered the quiet mountain paths, autumn was visible there.

I am deeply grateful to Ms. Ila Kim, the manager of the Book Cafe "Rephidim", who first introduced me to the beautiful place.

Ms. Ila Kim talked about the Seosan province as a sunset place. She recommended me to take the pathway, "Aramegil" along the eastern regions, Unsan and Haemi.

In winter, someone will be on the pathway of Aramegil that she would talk about.

In midsummer and fall in 2023,

차례

4 작가의 말 Author's Note
6 감사의 글 Acknowledgments

1부. 처음 들르고
First Passing by

14 동쪽 길 A Way to the East
16 읍내 벚꽃길 A Cherry Road
18 공원 수선화 Daffodils in the Park
20 동그라미 무지개 A Round Rainbow
22 벌천 물길 The Waterway
24 초원 오솔길 A Meadow Pathway
26 비 맞으며 Being in the Rain
28 한낮 안개비 A Drizzle at Midday
30 검은 머리끈 A Black Hair Band
32 개심사 들길 A Field to the Temple
34 서쪽 무지개 A Rainbow in the West
36 무지개 다리 A Rainbow Bridge

38 언덕 묘지 Tombs on the Hill
40 고풍마을 끝 The End of a Village
42 보원사 마당 The Site of Bowonsa Temple
44 보원사 계곡 A Valley at the Temple
46 마애불 미소 A Smile of Buddha

2부. 다시 한번 들르고
Passing by Again

50 서산 운산 길 For Seosan and Unsan
52 정말골 아래 A Village of Jungmalgol
54 운산 구름 The Clouds in Unsan
56 고풍호수 Gopung Lake
58 한겨울 그의 여동생 His Sister in Midwinter
60 냇가 따라서 Along a Stream
62 초록 저수지 A Green Reservoir
64 시드는 배롱나무 Withering Crape Myrtle
66 개심사 폭우 Rain at Gaesimsa Temple
68 댕댕이와 비탈길 A Puppy on the Slope
70 목장에 서서 Standing at the Ranch
72 곰실마을 서리태 Black Bean in the Field

74 아라메 느티나무 A Zelkova at Arame Park
76 느티나무 밤비 A Zelkova and Rain

3부. 가을이 보이고
Feeling the Season of Fall

80 수정봉 사과 Apples under the Peak
82 벌천 안개 Fog in the Stream
84 비 맞은 갈대 The Reeds in Rain
86 고향 가는 길 The Way Home
88 가을날 아침 One Morning in Fall
90 놀란 냇가 An Overflowing Stream
92 아라메 공원 At Arame Park
94 푸른 텃밭 A Green Garden
96 마음 여는 길 The Way to Open Mind
98 개심사 마당 The Yard of a Temple
100 개심사 공작단풍 A Maple Tree There
102 초원 너머에 Beyond the Meadow
104 가을 과수원 Apple Orchard in Fall
106 봉림마을 사과길 An Apple Road
108 붉은 봉림마을 The Red Village
110 대치리 장승 Totem Poles on Uphill

112 소나무 숲 The Pine Trees
114 사라진 소들 No Cows There
116 서리태 잎사귀 Leaves of Black Bean
118 빛나는 길 A Shining Path
120 골짜기 샘물 A Flow at the Valley
122 상왕산 바위 The Rocks in the Mountain

124 작품 해설 Work Comment

1부

처음 들르고

First Passing by

동쪽 길

서산 가는 길을
망설이다가

바로 오른쪽으로
조금 내려가면

운산 가는 길로
바로 이어지는데

이야기를 생각하고
들길을 지나가며

이야기를 생각하며
마을로 들어가고
냇가를 건너가네.

A Way to the East

Hesitating for a while
On the road to Seosan,

Going down a little
To the right side,

It soon connects
To the way to Unsan.

Thinking of the stories
I pass through the fields.

Thinking of the stories
I go into the small town,
And cross the stream.

읍내 벚꽃길

운산 읍내 큰길로
들어가지 않아도

오른쪽 작은 길로
비켜서 들어가면

어찌나 반가운지
벚나무 늘어서네.

이른 봄날에는
벚꽃 터져나고

찬바람 불어대면
읍내로 날리다가

들길 따라가며
구름 되어 흩날리네.

A Cherry Road

Not going into the town
Through the main road,

Going into the town
Through the small road,

I can see the cherries
Lining up the road.

On an early spring day,
The blossoms burst out.

When the cold wind blows,
They are flying into town.

Following the field,
They scatter forming clouds.

공원 수선화

수선화 심어 놓은
아라메 공원에

강아지풀 머리 내밀고
바랭이풀 길게 자라고
뽕나무 줄기 나오는데

잡초에 뒤섞여도
수선화 줄기 여전하네.

내년 봄이 되면
노랗게 피어나서

아라메 봄바람에
한들한들 끄덕이겠지

Daffodils in the Park

The daffodils are planted
In Arame Park.

Foxtail sticks out its head,
Indica grass grows long,
Mulberry trunks appear,

Being mixed up in the weeds,
The daffodil stems are still.

In the spring next year,
They'll bloom yellow.

In the spring breeze,
The daffodils will nod.

동그라미 무지개

하늘에 그려진
동그라미

빗방울 떨어지며
날리고

빗방울 날리며
구르고

빗방울 구르며
다시 날리고

빗방울 찍어서
하늘에 그리는데
동그라미 무지개

A Round Rainbow

Drawn in the sky,
It's a round.

Falling raindrops,
Flying

Flying raindrops,
Rolling down.

Rolling down raindrops,
Blowing it again.

Taking raindrops,
Drawing them in the sky,
It's a round rainbow.

벌천 물길

수정봉 샘물 한줄기
고원사 마당 지나고

계곡 바위 닿으며
한없이 맑아지네.

고풍호수에 담겨서
한없이 깊어지고
한동안 머물다가

조금씩 흐르고
느리게 흘러서
벌천으로 내려가네.

서쪽으로 흐르는데
서산 바다로 가겠네.

The Waterway

A stream from Sujeongbong
Passes the yard of Gowonsa.

Reaching the rocks in valley,
It becomes brilliantly clearer.

Gathering in Gopung Lake,
It gets infinitely deeper
Staying there for a while.

It flows little by little,
Flows slowly and
Goes down to Beolcheon.

It flows to the west and
Will reach the sea in Seosan.

초원 오솔길

푸른 초원 안에서
언덕 너머 숲까지
오솔길 나 있는데

한 명 지나가고
두 명 지나가고
세 명 지나가는데

언덕에 올라가면
파란 하늘 더 높고
흰 구름 더 멀지만

앞서가던 사람들은
어디로 가려는지
말없이 걸어가네.

A Meadow Pathway

In the green meadows,
Beyond the hill and forest,
There is a pathway.

One person passes by,
Two people pass by,
Three people are passing by.

When going up the hill,
The blue sky is higher;
The white clouds are away.

Those who were ahead,
Where they are going to,
Walking without a word.

비 맞으며

오늘 비 내리면
길을 가다가 맞아요.

산에도 내리는데
들에도 내리는데

마지막 여름비
서늘하게 내려요.

다음에 또 내려서
길을 가다가 맞으면

산도 싸늘하고
들도 싸늘하고

Being in the Rain

If it rains today,
I will meet it on the path.

It'll fall on the mountain
And in the fields.

The last summer rain
Will cool down.

If it falls again next time,
I'll be in it on the way.

It'll cool the forests,
It'll cold the fields.

한낮 안개비

한낮에도 안개비
자욱하게 내려서

산바람 타고서
푸른 들판까지
촉촉이 적셔서
들안개 일어나네.

잠시 걸어가는데
들길이 젖어 들고

머리도 젖어 들고
마음도 젖어 들어
발길을 다시 돌리네.

A Drizzle at Midday

Fog and rain in the midday
Are falling thickly.

Riding the mountain breeze,
Soaking with moist
To the green fields,
A wild fog is rising up.

When I walk for a while,
The fields are getting wet.

My head is wet;
My heart also gets wet;
I turn my steps again.

검은 머리끈

검은 머리끈 하나가
마당에 떨어져 있기에
망설이다가 주워 들었네.

가늘고 동그란 머리끈인데
손가락으로 당겨보고는
바지 주머니에 넣어두네.

어찌 생각해 보면
이곳에 떨어진 머리끈을
다시 찾아보겠다고
둘러보는 이도 없을 테고

다시 생각해 보니
여기에 오가던 사람들은
오직 나밖에 없으니

내 바지 주머니에서
우연히 떨어졌겠지.

A Black Hair Band

Seeing a black hair band
In the yard of a park,
I hesitate and pick it up.

The thin, round hair band.
I pull it with my finger
And keep it in my pocket.

If I think about it,
None will come again
To find it out here.

On second thought,
Nobody came here
Without me for walking.

It might fell by accident
In my pants pocket.

개심사 들길

개심사 가는 길에
옆으로 눈길을 돌리네.

벼 들길 따라가며
배롱나무 세어 보고

언덕 둑길 오르면
호수 물결 조용하고

호수 언저리 따라가면
목장 풀밭 경사지고

산 한 굽이 지나는데
이내 소나기 쏟아지고

마지막 한 굽이까지
줄곧 소나기 쏟아지고

개심사: 충남 서산시 운산군 지역의 사찰

A Field to the Temple

On the way to Gaesimsa
I'm looking to the side.

Following the rice fields,
Count the crape myrtle trees.

On the hill of a causeway,
Lake ripples are quiet.

On the edge of the lake,
A ranch meadow is sloping.

Passing by a bend of the hill,
Soon a shower pours down.

Until going to the last curve,
It's raining all the time.

Gaesimsa Temple: A historic temple in Unsan area, Seosan.

서쪽 무지개

빗방울 날아가면
허전할까봐.

파란 하늘 드러나면
허전하여서

하얀 구름 흩어지면
허전하여서

크고 연하게
무지개 그려 놓았네.

서쪽 하늘이 비어서
그렇게 허전할까봐.

A Rainbow in the West

When raindrops fly,
The sky feels empty.

When the blue sky appears,
It feels lonesome.

When the clouds disperse,
It feels lonesome.

A big and soft rainbow
The sky draws in the sky.

The western sky is filled,
For it feels so empty.

무지개 다리

무지개는 하늘을
반으로 가르는데

사랑하는 분들은
무지개 다리를
건너가시고

무지개 아래에는
슬픔이 남아있고

무지개 위에는
슬픈 색깔이
하늘을 가로지르고

A Rainbow Bridge

A rainbow in the sky
Is cutting it in half.

Those who love
Are crossing over
A rainbow bridge.

Under the rainbow
There remains sadness.

Above the rainbow
The sad colors
Are crossing the sky.

언덕 묘지

고풍호수 올라가면
비탈 언저리 지나서
산길 옆 돋은 터에

저수지 담겨진 물살
빤히 내려다 보이네.

햇살 들어서 아담하고
잔디 깔끔히 자라는데
봉분들이 안 보이네

오랫동안 안식하고
최근에 옮겨졌는지

가을 햇살 따가운데
묘지 주인은 가시고

Tombs on the Hill

Going up to the Gopung Lake,
Passing the edge of the slope,
The raised ground by the path,

Water flow in reservoir
Can be seen right down.

It's nice and sunny,
The grass grows neatly,
No mounds can be seen.

After resting for a long time,
They may have been moved.

Autumn sunlight are blazing;
The residents have gone.

고풍마을 끝

고풍저수지 옆길로
산비탈 돌아가면

산속 끝 마을에
버스정거장 있는데
기다리는 이는 없고

저수지 비탈 아래
들깨 덤불 자라서
뒷산 골짜기까지
무성하게 오르는데

쓰러진 줄기 세우고
솎아내는 이도 없고

한 집 건너 옆집은
무너져서 비어 있네.

The End of a Village

To the path by the pond
If you go to the valley,

At the end of a village,
There is a bus stop,
Even no one waiting.

Below the slope of the pond,
Perilla bushes grow.

To the valley behind the hill,
They're rising lushly.

There is none to thin it out,
To lift up the fallen trunks.

One house by the next door
Has collapsed and vacant.

보원사 마당

용현계곡 지나며
물소리 이어져도
산으로 막혀있네.

물소리 잠잠하면
산길이 열려지고
산바람 불어오네.

당간지주 우뚝하고
사찰 마당 지나서

개울을 건너가면
오층석탑 웅장하고

사찰 석축 뒤편에
선사 부도탑 나란히
선사 신도비 나란히

보원사: 충남 서산시 운산군 지역의 무너진 사찰

The Site of Bowonsa Temple

Passing through the Yonghyeon Valley,
The sound of water is go on,
Yet the path is blocked by mountains.

The sound of water is quiet;
The path is open;
The wind is blow in.

Stone pillar is standing tall
Across the temple yard.

Crossing the stream,
The five-story stone pagoda is grand.

Over the stone wall of the yard,
Stand a stupa of the most reverend
Facing a stele of the most reverend.

Bowonsa Temple: A historic temple site in Unsan area, Seosan.

보원사 계곡

물소리 들으며
갈참나무 푸르고

물소리 들으며
단풍나무 푸르고

한두 달 지나서
계절이 바뀌면

갈참나무 물들고
단풍나무 물들고

걸어가는 발길도
점점 물들어 가고

A Valley at the Temple

Hearing the sound of water,
The oak trees are green.

Hearing the sound of water,
Maple trees are green.

After a month or two,
The seasons are changed.

The oak trees are dyed;
Maple trees change color.

The steps through the path
Are getting colored.

마애불 미소

어느 날 해질 때
서산으로 해질 때

마애불 얼굴에
가을바람 스치면

마애불 수줍어서
어쩔 줄 모르고

해지는 줄 모르고
빙긋 웃기만 하고

해지는 줄 알아도
빙긋 웃기만 하고

A Smile of Buddha

One day the sun sets,
Going down to Seosan.

On the face on the cliff,
The autumn wind passes.

The Buddha seems shy
Hesitating what to do.

Without realizing sunset,
It wears a smile.

Even realizing sunset,
It wears a smile.

2부

다시 한번 들르고
Passing by Again

서산 운산 길

큰길을 따라가면
서산으로 들어가고

옆길로 나오면
운산으로 가는데

서산으로 가려다가
운산으로 나가는데

동쪽을 얼핏 보니
산자락 보이기에

산 위에 머무르는
구름이 부르기에

For Seosan and Unsan

Following the main road,
Entering Seosan, a big city:

Coming out to the side way,
Going to Unsan, a small town:

In spite of going to Seosan,
Choosing to go to Unsan.

A quick glance to the east
Leads the foot of mountain.

Clouds staying over the peak,
Are calling me there.

정말골 아래

정말골 들어가면
정든 이들 모이고
정든 이들 살아서

상왕산 아래에는
정든 이야기 들리고

서쪽 산 바라보며
너른 들 펼쳐져서

가던 길을 돌려서
정말골로 들어가요.

A Village of Jungmalgol

If you go down the valley,
Those who are sweet gather;
Those who are sweet live.

Down Sangwangsan peak,
Sweet stories are heard.

Staring at the western hill,
Wide fields spread out.

Turning around the way,
A wanderer goes the village.

운산 구름

구름이 모이고
구름이 머물고
구름이 지나가는데

서쪽 너머로
아름다운 서산으로
서서히 넘어가네.

구름 마을이어서
사람도 모이고
사연도 쌓여서

구름 마을 안에는
사람은 떠났어도
사연이 떠오르고

The Clouds in Unsan

The clouds are gathering,
The clouds are staying,
The clouds are passing by.

Beyond the west hill,
To the beautiful Seosan,
The clouds go by slowly.

In the cloud village,
People gather together
Stories are piled up.

Inside the cloud village,
Though people left there,
Stories come to mind.

고풍호수

산봉우리 서너 개
한꺼번에 담고서
깊은 골짝 이루고

가파른 큰 바위를
한꺼번에 담아서
큰 절벽 만들었네.

산봉우리 아래로
바위 절벽 아래로

계곡도 가라앉고
살던 터전 잠기고
이야기도 잠기고

Gopung Lake

Three or four peaks,
Putting them all together
Are forming a deep valley.

Steep big rocks,
Putting them all together
Are building a big cliff.

Down the peaks,
Down the rock cliff,

The valley is submerged;
The residences are sunk;
The stories are also sunk.

한겨울 그의 여동생

한겨울 추운 날에
친구 여동생이 시집간 곳은

좁은 고개를 지나가서
왼쪽 언덕에 농장이 있었는데

어쩌다 소문에 듣기로는
소들을 키운다고 했는데
힘들게 고생한다고도 했는데

이미 어머니도 돌아가시고
그 오빠도 먼 길로 가셨는데
여동생은 어찌 살았는지

운산에 살았는지
운산에 살고 있는지
운산을 떠났는지

운산에 구름은 떠 있어도
삶의 자취는 사라지고

His Sister in Midwinter

On a cold day in midwinter,
The place where she married off
Was a farm over a narrow hill.

From what I heard by chance,
She might raise cows
Going through a hard time.

Her mother passed away;
Her brother has also died,
How does she live?

Did she live in Unsan?
Does she live in Unsan?
Has she left in Unsan?

Being clouds floating in Unsan,
The trace of her life has gone.

냇가 따라서

용장마을 길에서
개울을 바라보면

너른 둑길 따라서
잡초가 무성하고

둑길 아래로
물 흐름 더디고

물새들 지나가며
일부러 내려앉네.

들판을 지나려다
잠시 쉬어 가려고

Along a Stream

On the path of a village,
The stream can be seen,

Along the wide causeway,
Lush weeds can be seen.

Down the causeway,
The water flow is slow.

Water birds passing by
Are often falling down.

Passing through a field,
They may take a break.

초록 저수지

늦여름 고풍저수지
한가지 색깔

물속도 초록
물가도 초록

뒷산 봉오리
옆산 능선
온통 초록빛

호수 둘러진 나무들
배수로 입구 벗나무
진하고 진한 초록빛

A Green Reservoir

Gopung Lake in late summer
Is one color.

Green in deep water,
Green in waterside.

A peak behind the mountain,
A ridge next mountain,
Everything is green.

The trees surrounding the lake,
Cherry trees near the drain
Are dark, dark green.

시드는 배롱나무

울타리 장식하며
백일이나 빛나더니

가을이 오려는지
붉은 빛이 시들었네.

한동안 데우더니
서서히 가라앉고서

꽃잎이 떨어지니
한 계절 지나가네

백일이나 빛나더니
얼마나 지쳤는지

Withering Crape Myrtle

Decorating the fence
It has shined for 100 days.

Fall is about to come,
The red light has faded.

After heating it for a while,
It is slowly sinking.

As the petals fall,
A season passes by.

It has shined for 100 days
How exhausted it has been!

개심사 폭우

별안간 폭우 내리고
산 주변 빗물 줄기
모여들어서 흐르고

빗물이 철철 거리니
발길 내딛기 어려워
나무 아래 비켜서네.

성난 빗발 내리면서
천둥소리 울리는데

하나라도 남김없이
쓸어내려고 정했네.

무어라도 담지 말고
씻고 흘려서 비우고

이런저런 생각들도
빗물에 흘려보내고
빗물조차도 버리고

Rain at Gaesimsa Temple

Heavy rain suddenly falls
Rainwater around the woods
Gathers and flows away.

The rain is pouring down;
It's hard to take a step,
Standing under the tree.

With angry rain falling
There's a sound of thunder.

Nothing is left behind,
It decides to sweep away.

Nothing permits to put it in,
It washes for nothing,

Something or others
Let them flow in the rain,
Even the rainwater itself.

댕댕이와 비탈길

한 굽이 돌아가면
들어가는데

한 고개 넘어가면
들어가는데

거기에서 되돌아서
다시 내려가네.

댕댕이 피곤하여
품 속에 안고서
다시 내려가네.

저 너머 그곳을
마음 속에 담고서
다음에 들르기를

A Puppy on the Slope

Turning one bend of a hill
Reaches the temple.

Going over one hill
Reaches there.

However, I stop there
And go back down.

The puppy is tired,
So holding it in my arms
I go back down.

That place beyond the hill
Holding in my heart,
I hope to stop by later.

목장에 서서

목장을 지나가면
발길을 멈추고서
초원을 바라보네.

소들이 안 보여도
소들을 기다리네.

언덕 너머에서
소들이 오기를
한동안 기다리네.

하늘에 구름이
이리로 몰려오면

초원에 소들이
이리로 넘어오기를

Standing by the Ranch

Passing the ranch,
Stopping my way,
I look at the meadow.

Not being cows seen there
I wait for them appearing.

Over the far hill side,
Hoping cows come down,
I'm waiting for a while.

When clouds in the sky
Gather here,

Cows in the meadow
Will come over here.

곰실마을 서리태

고산리 길 따라서
곰실마을 들어가면

보이는 데마다
서리태 자라는데

좁은 길가에도
밭둑 비탈에도

알뜰하게 총총하게
서리태 심으셨네.

가을에 서리 내리면
어느 분이 거두려나?

Black Bean in the Field

Going along the Gosanri path
Will lead you to Gomsil village.

Everywhere you see,
Black bean is growing.

Even on the narrow road,
On the slope of the field,

Attentively and thoroughly,
They planted the plant.

When frost falls in the fall,
Who will harvest the plant?

아라메 느티나무

느티나무 오래되면
큰 기둥은 파이고
비어서 삭아 들고

나무가지 쳐지고
꺾여서 기우는데

아라메 느티나무는
600년 지났다는데
기둥이 당당하네.

구름 아래 푸르고
사방으로 퍼져서
줄기마다 의젓하네.

A Zelkova at Arame Park

The zelkova tree gets older,
The pillar tends to be rotten,
Empty, and withering away.

Tree branches also fall,
Being bent and tilted.

A zelkova at Arame Park
May be over 600 years old,
The pillar looks strong.

Being blue under the clouds,
Spreading out in all sides,
Every stem keep with dignity.

느티나무 밤비

느티나무 나뭇잎이
소란하게 비벼대니

한밤중에
사나운 바람 불면서
소나기 쏟아졌는데

아침에는
하늘이 마냥 높으니
소나기 그쳤는데

잠시 후에
하얀 구름 바라보면
눈이 부시겠네.

A Zelkova and Rain

Zelkova tree leaves
Are rubbing loudly.

In the midnight,
With a fierce wind,
It was raining.

In the morning,
With the so high sky,
The shower stopped.

After a while,
When the white clouds,
It must be dazzling.

3부

가을이 보이고

Feeling the Season of Fall

산 아래 사과나무

수정봉 산기슭은
너무나도 깊어서
들어가지 못하고

산 아래 언덕마다
사과나무 심었네.

무더운 한여름에
데워지고 익어서

서늘한 가을날에
단단히 굳어지고

수정봉 색깔대로
붉게 타들어 가네.

Apple Trees under the Hill

The peak of Sujeongbong
Is so deep and steep,
Does not permit to go up.

On the foot of the hill,
Apple trees was planted.

In the hot midsummer,
Apples are warmed and ripen.

On a cool fall day,
They hardens slowly.

Imitating the color of the hill,
Apples are getting red.

벌천 안개

벌천 한 가운데
안개에 잠겨서
물길을 가리고

냇가 둑길에는
가을비 내리며
벚나무 적시네.

냇물이 흐르며
가을이 흘러가고
사연을 보내는데

벌천 안개에 가려서
사연은 알 수 없네.

Fog in the Stream

In the middle of the stream,
The waterway is immersed,
Covered in fog.

On the bank of the stream,
Autumn rain is falling,
Wetting the cherry trees.

As the stream flows
Autumn is passing by
Sending some stories.

However, covered in fog,
It does not tell the stories.

비 맞은 갈대

모처럼 가을비는
며칠이나 내려서

수정봉 갈래마다
산안개 오르는데

보원사 마당부터
계곡 물살 빠르고
고풍호수 넘치네.

벌천 물길 넓어져서
물가 잡초 쓰러져도
갈대 줄기는 퍼지네.

The Reeds in Rain

The rain in autumn
Has been falling for days.

In the valleys of Sujeongbong,
The fog is rising.

From the yard of Bowonsa,
The current is fast,
Gopung Lake is overflowing.

The waterway has widened,
The weeds fall down,
The reeds are spreading.

고향 가는 길

이른 아침에
조금 빠르게
길을 나섰지만

큰길도 밀리고
좁은 길도 밀리고

가도 가도 밀리다가
어느덧 길이 훤하네.

들길로 들어서고
가을이 보이고

들길을 지나가면
가을 소리 들리고

The Way Home

Early in the morning,
A little faster,
I went out on the road.

Even main road is tied up,
Narrow road is tied up.

Waiting, waiting for a while,
The road is finally clear.

Entering the field road,
Fall is clearly seen.

Passing through the field,
The sound of fall is heard.

가을날 아침

잠시 기다리다가
모르게 잠이 들고

잠결에 일어나서
창문을 닫아두고

새벽에 깨어보니
가을이 되었네.

하루 더 지나면
가을밤이 오는데

서늘하지 않아도
창문을 닫아야지.

One Morning in Fall

After waiting for a while,
I fell asleep in spite of myself.

Waking up in my sleep,
Leaving the window closed,

After waking up at dawn
It's already fall.

After one more day,
Autumn night is coming.

Though it's not cool,
The window needs closing.

놀란 냇가

벌천 냇물이 넘실거려
빠르게 몰려서 흐르니

물가 촘촘하던 갈대들
하루 사이에 쓸려갔네.

저 위에 고풍호수에
무슨 일이 있나 보다.

며칠 밤낮으로
큰비 내리더니

보원사 숲속에서
짐승들은 잠 못 들고

고풍호수 담긴 물이
너무나 무거웠나 보다.

An Overflowing Stream

The stream is overflowing,
Flowing quickly.

The reeds close to the water
Are sweeping away in a day.

Up there at Gopung Lake,
Something may be going on.

For several days and nights,
It has rained heavily.

In the forest of Bowonsa,
Wild animals couldn't sleep.

Water in Gopung Lake
Might be too heavy.

아라메 공원

아라메 공원에는
느티나무 잎사귀
높아서 한들대고

다홍색 꽃무릇
낮아서 한들대고

이웃에 둘러 진 집들
낮은 담장에 그려진
꽃들도 한들대고

무궁화 담장
해바라기 담장
코스모스 담장
구절초 담장

벽화 속에서도
한가로이 한들대고

At Arame Park

At Arame Park
The leaves of zelkova tree
Are wavering so high.

A bunch of reddish lycoris
Is wavering so low.

Flowers painted on low walls
Of neighboring houses
Are also fluttering.

Wall of sharons
Wall of sunflowers
Wall of cosmoses
Wall of daisies,

On the walls of houses,
Flowers are waving leisurely.

푸른 텃밭

벌천 둑길 옆으로
파란 양철지붕 집에
담장 벽화 그려지고

울타리 없는 텃밭은
한사람이 여유롭게
가꾸어 낼 크기로서
한 평 반 정도인데

서리태 한 고랑
생강 두 고랑 푸르고

아욱 한 고랑
대파 두 고랑 푸르고

A Green Garden

Next to Beolcheon causeway,
At a house of blue tin roof,
A mural is painted.

A garden without a fence
Is about ten or so feet
For a person to cultivate
Spending some hours off.

All furrows are green:
One furrow of soybean,
Two furrows of ginger,
One furrow of mallow,
Two furrows of green onion.

마음 여는 길

남쪽 들녘 바라보며
갈산마을에서 오르고

목초지 곱게 깔려진
초록마을 들어서면

개망초 시들거리고
벼 이삭은 익어가네.

운벌리 고개길에
소들을 찾아보다가

산바람 내려온다는
신창마을로 내려가네.

마음을 열어주는
마음을 열어야 하는
개심사 길로 들어가네.

개심사 (開心寺): 마음을 열어주는 의미, 또는 마음을 열어야 한다는 의미를 가진 사찰

The Way to Open Mind

Looking at the southern fields,
Climbing from Galsan Village,

Seeing beautiful pasture,
I enter the green village,

The fleabane is withering,
The ears of rice are ripening.

On the slope of Unberley,
Looking for cows in the fields,
Where breeze is coming down,
I go down to Sinchang Village.

I'm entering the way to Gaesimsa,
Opening my inner mind,
Or to need opening mind.

The Gaesimsa Temple (開心寺): The name of the ancient temple means that we should open our mind or our mind should be open.

개심사 마당

누각 축대 아래
계곡 물소리 들리고

배롱나무 꽃잎도
어느덧 시들었네.

네모난 연못에는
작은 연잎 떠 있고

초록 나무 둘러져
쑥색으로 탁한데

맑기를 바라지 말고
스스로 맑아야 하나?

마음의 눈을 열어야
맑게 보이게 되려나?

The Yard of a Temple

Under the stone embankment,
The valley water is heard.

The petals of crape myrtle
Have been withered.

In the square pond,
There are lotus leaves floating.

Surrounded by green trees,
The pond is dark green.

Instead of hoping to be clear,
Should I clear myself?

If we open our inner eyes,
Shall we be clear ourselves?

개심사 공작단풍

범종각 한켠에
돌축대 옆에서
잔뜩 움츠리네.

기둥은 자라다가
두어 번 휘어지고

잎사귀는 아래로
우산처럼 내리고

옆에 자란 벚나무
일찌감치 시들어서
잎사귀 떨어지니

햇빛이 들게 되면
불그레 물들겠지.

A Maple Tree There

On one side of a pavilion
Next to the stone steps,
It curls itself up.

The stem grows
Bending a couple of times.

The leaves are down
Falling like an umbrella.

The cherry leaves next to it
Withered away early,
And the leaves are falling.

If it gets the sunlight,
The maple will turn red.

초원 너머에

멀리서 멈추어서
목장을 바라보면

소들이 무리 지어
두리번 거리면서
이리저리 거닐던데.

가까이 가서 보면
목장 울타리 안에는
푸른 풀밭만 깔리고

소들은 저 너머로
어디론가 가버렸네.

다시 멀리 가서는
목장을 바라보며는
소들은 나오려는지.

Beyond the Meadow

Stopping from afar
If I look at the ranch,

A herd of cows
Wandering around there
Are walking around.

If I come to be closer,
There is only green grass
Inside the ranch fence,

And the cows are gone
Over somewhere else.

Going far again
If I look at the ranch,
Are the cows coming out?

가을 과수원

가을 이슬은
곳곳에 스며들어
사과를 적시고

가을 햇살은
곳곳을 비추면서
사과를 익히고

하루하루 무거워서
하루하루 붉어지고

볼수록 무거워서
볼수록 붉어지고

Apple Orchard in Fall

The chill dew of fall
Permeating everywhere,
Soaks the apples.

The sunlight of fall
Shining everywhere,
Ripens apples.

Being heavy every day,
They are getting redder.

The heavier it gets;
The redder it becomes.

봉림마을 사과길

산으로 둘러져서
나무들 빼곡한데

산길 고개 넘어서
저 아래 저수지까지
길 따라서 내려가면

길가에 알알이 매달린
붉은 사과 마을이네.

사과 익어 가는 곳으로
천천히 내려가야 하네.

다시 되돌아 올라가도
사과 익어가는 길

An Apple Road

Surrounded by mountains
They are covered with forest.

Over the mountain road
To the reservoir below,

If you go down the road,
They are full of apple trees
On the roadside of the village.

To the place apples ripen,
You can go down slowly.

Though you go back up again,
Apples are ripen on the side.

붉은 봉림마을

원평마을 고개 넘어서
수창봉 산길 내려가면

울타리 안에도
울타리 밖에도

줄지어 서 있는
가을 나무들

작은 나무에도
키 큰 나무에도
붉어지는 사과들

무거워 매달린 사과들
가을 담은 사과들

The Red Village

Beyond the hill of a village
When you go down the path,

Even inside the fence,
Even outside the fence,
Autumn trees line up.

Even on small trees,
Even in tall trees,
Apples are turning red.

Apples hanging in the trees
Hold the season of fall.

대치리 장승들

대치리 고개길에
장승들 서 있는데

옛날에 모셔졌던
나무장승 두 개는
뒤쪽에 물러나고

언젠가 새로 만든
돌장승 두 개는
앞쪽에 세워졌네.

돌장승 또 하나에
대치리 새겨놓고
운산 예산 알리네

장승들을 보면서
나그네들 지나고
스님들도 지나고

Totem Poles on Uphill

On the uphill pass in Daechi-ri
The totem poles are standing.

Enshrined in the past
Two wooden poles
Retreat to the back.

Built someday in a little later
Two stone poles
Were erected in the front.

Another stone pole
Engraved Daechi-ri, this village,
Tells the ways, Unsan and Yesan.

Looking at the poles,
The travelers have passed by,
The monks have also passed by.

소나무 숲

개심사 소나무
곳곳이 자라서

붉그런 기둥은
창처럼 서 있네.

솔잎이 퍼져서
하늘을 가리고
구름도 가리고

솔잎이 떨어져
솔밭을 이루고
쉼터를 이루고

The Pine Trees

Pine trees at the temple
Are growing everywhere.

The red pillars
Are standing like spears.

Pine needles spread out
Covering the sky
Covering the clouds.

Pine needles are falling,
Form a pine field,
And create a shelter.

사라진 소들

초원을 바라보면
넓게만 이어지고
소들을 안 보이네.

초원 언덕 넘어서
어디로 갔나 보네.

지난 계절에는
풀밭만 무성하고

이번 계절에는
초원 시들어 가도
소들은 안 보이네.

어느 계절에 오면
소들이 나오려는지.

No Cows There

In a vacant meadow
Which stretches widely,
No cows can be seen.

Beyond the meadow hill
They may wander away.

In the last season
Only the grass was lush.

In this season
Even the grassland withers,
No cows can be seen.

In what season
Are the cows coming out?

서리태 잎사귀

들길 옆에 노란 벼는
일찍 여물어 가다가

서리 내리기 전에
지난주에 베어지고
넓은 평야 남겨지고

서리태 누런 잎사귀
따가운 햇살 맞으며
날마다 시들어 가네.

며칠 더 지나가서
차가운 밤공기 쐬며
서리 맞아야 하기에

The Leaves of Black Bean

Yellow rice next to the field
Was ripening early.

Before falling the frost
It was cut down last week,
A wide plain is left behind.

The leaves of the bean
In the warm sunlight
Were withering every day.

For a few more days
The bean needs breathing
And frost in cold night air.

빛나는 길

벌천 냇가에서
갈대 희게 빛나더니

가루고개 지나며
억새풀 희게 빛나고

신창마을 가까이
구절초 희게 빛나네.

홍천 개울 길에
댑싸리 붉게 빛나고

개심사 들어가며
엄나무 붉게 빛나네.

A Shining Path

At Beolcheon stream,
The reeds shine brightly.

Passing through Garu uphill,
Silver grasses shine whit.

Near Sinchang village,
Daisies shine white.

On Hongcheon stream,
Broom cypress shine red.

Entering Gaesimsa Temple,
The moth trees shine red.

골짜기 샘물

개심사 계곡물은
돌 틈을 두드리며
조용히 흐르다가

돌 사이 여울에
단풍잎 담아 놓네

일주문 지나가면
물소리 작아지고

가랑잎 담아내는
흐름조차 마르고

솔숲 길 돌아가면
가랑잎에 덮이고

A Flow at the Valley

The water at Gaesimsa Valley
Knocking on the cracks,
Flows quietly.

In the shallows between stones,
It holds maple leaves.

After passing the main gate,
The sound of water gets quiet.

Filled with leaves,
The flow finally dries up.

Returning to the pine forest,
The leaves cover the flow.

상왕산 바위

수천 년 비바람에
바위가 쪼개지고
계곡이 파여지고

수백 년 비바람에
바위가 굴러내려
계곡이 깊어지고

한 계절 비바람에
고목이 넘어지고
산길이 무너지고

하루밤 비바람에
가랑잎 떨어지고
마음이 흔들리고

The Rocks in the Mountain

For thousands of years,
The rocks split;
The valley was dug out.

For hundreds of years,
The rocks rolled down;
The valley got deeper.

For one season of a year,
The old tree fell down;
The narrow path collapsed.

For one night,
The leaves are falling;
My mind seems changing.

작품 해설

- 아라메 둘레길에서 아름다운 운산, 빛나는 서산 이야기 -

심재황
영어학 박사, 언어와 문화, 문화연구

　서산 지역의 입구에 운산이 있으며, 서산으로 들어가는 길에서 그곳의 산을 바라보게 된다. 잠시라도 여유를 가지려면 들러보고 싶은 고장이다. 아니면 조금 들어가다가 바로 되돌아 나와도 되는 곳이다.
　작가는 누구에게 들었는지 일단 동쪽 운산 지역으로 들어가기로 한다. 따라서 작가의 이야기는 여기에서 시작되고 있다.

> 서산 가는 길을
> 망설이다가
>
> 바로 오른쪽으로
> 조금 내려가면
>
> 운산 가는 길로
> 바로 이어지는데
>
> 　　　　　　-동쪽 길- 중에서

그런데 일단 그곳에 들어가 보면 우리에게 친숙한 곳들이 여기저기 산재해 있는데, 하나 같이 정겨운 길을 지나고 있다. 작은 읍내를 벗어나면 우선 남쪽으로 향하게 된다. 읍내를 흐르는 벌천 냇가를 따라가거나 건너가거나, 아니면 읍내 바로 옆으로 빠져나가는 정겨운 길이 보인다.

운산 읍내 큰길로
들어가지 않아도

오른쪽 작은 길로
비켜서 들어가면

어찌나 반가운지
벚나무 늘어서네.

-읍내 벗길- 중에서

운산면에서 남쪽 가면 해미 읍성이 있다. 그 길에 유서 깊은 개심사를 들르게 된다. 또 그전에는 조선시대 명종대왕 태실을 모신 태봉마을이 있으며, 이 일대에는 우리의 눈길을 멀리까지 끌게 하는 목장 초원들이 넓고 높이 이어져 있다.

개심사 가는 길에
옆으로 눈길을 돌리네.

벼 들길 따라가며
배롱나무 세어 보고

언덕 둑길 오르면
호수 물결 조용하고

호수 언저리 따라가면
목장 풀밭 경사지고

-개심사 들길- 중에서

 물론 상왕산 골짜기마다 마을들이 들어가 있는데, 알려주는 마을 이름들도 정다움을 담고 있다. 비록 그 옛날 삶의 모습은 변화되었지만, 그나마 그 이름으로 옛날의 흔적이 남겨져 있다고 생각된다.
 읍내에서 남쪽으로 가는 길에서 동쪽 언덕으로 올라가면 고풍호수에 이르게 된다. 산에서 나온 물을 담아 놓은 저수지인데, 호수를 둘러싸고 있는 골짜기들로 인하여, 한눈에 보이지 않기에 빙글 들러보게 된다.
 호수 둘레를 따라가면 꼬리가 긴 큰 물고기 모양임을 알 수 있다. 그런데 그 지역 마을에서는 호수의 모양을 호수에서 움직이는 용의 형상이라고 말하고 있다.

산봉우리 아래로
바위 절벽 아래로

계곡도 가라앉고
살던 터전 잠기고
이야기도 잠기고

-고풍호수- 중에서

꼬리 부분 지역은 두 군데로 이어지는데, 한 곳은 용현계곡에서 들어가게 된다. 다른 한 곳은 고풍마을 위를 지나가는데, 고개길을 넘어서 덕산 지역 봉림마을로 이어진다.

이 두 갈래 길은 모두 수정봉 골짜기에서 갈라져 나오고 있다. 한 줄기는 깊은 용현계곡으로 이어지고, 그 계곡에는 유서 깊은 고원사 터전과 유적이 있다. 그리고 한쪽 골짜기에는 너무나도 아름다운 미소를 품고 있는 서산 마애삼존불이 모셔져 있다.

> 어느 날 해질 때
> 서산으로 해질 때
>
> 마애불 얼굴에
> 가을바람 스치면
>
> 마애불 수줍어서
> 어쩔 줄 모르고
>
> -마애불 미소- 중에서

또 다른 한 줄기는 수창봉 고개를 넘어서 덕산 지방의 봉림마을 아래로 내려간다. 이 고장은 운산이나 서산과 다른 정취를 담고 있다. 수정봉에서 반사된 햇살은 과수원 사과에 그대로 담겨 있는 고장이다.

다시 말해서, 높은 수정봉 줄기에서 이어지는 수창봉 고개에서 저 아래 봉림저수지까지 사과 과수원 길이 계속되고 있다. 작가는 가을에 익어가는 사과에 대한 정감을 실제로 가을 산의 모습과 대비하여 묘사하고 있다.

무더운 한여름에
데워지고 익어서

서늘한 가을날에
단단히 굳어지고

수정봉 색깔대로
붉게 타들어 가네.

-산 아래 사과나무- 중에서

 작가는 이러한 지역을 다니면서 그 고장에 남아있는 자연의 모습들을 작품으로 남기고 있다. 다시 말해서, 작가의 시에는 지역적인 정취와 함께 자연에 대한 사랑이 그대로 담겨 있다.
 그리고 사라져 가는 우리의 문화와 전통에 대한 아쉬움을 사실적이면서 서정적으로 그려내고 있다. 다음 글에서도 작가의 정서가 우리에게 친숙하게 전해지기를 기대한다.